MEMORIES
OF
WALSALL

ALTON DOUGLAS
DENNIS MOORE
ADDITIONAL RESEARCH BY JO DOUGLAS

Published by Brewin Books Ltd, Doric House, Church Street, Studley, Warwickshire. B80 7LG.

Printed by Heron Press, Unit 19, Bilton Ind. Est., Stockmans Close, Kings Norton, Birmingham B38 9TS.

ISBN No. 1 85858 116 8

CONTENTS

INTRODUCTION

Early records reveal about fifty forms of the name WALSALL, although the Domesday Book (1086 AD) strangely makes no mention of the town, yet other smaller places like Bloxwich are noted. The earliest recorded spelling takes the form of Walesho (1004 AD) and it is not until 1484 that we meet the name in its present form. The derivation is considered by some as "the hall (abode) of the Welsh (or stranger)", by others as "the abode in the woods" (and remember that forests were widespread at the time), and yet again "the hall of Wealh", probably the name of a chieftain.

Walsall cannot claim by any means to be of great historical importance, unlike nearby Coventry, Birmingham, Worcester and others, but it can certainly claim, in fairly modern times, that it has developed immensely as a town of manufacturing and industrial stature. Population figures are always a good measure of the progress of any town. The census of 1801 gives a figure of 10,399. Forty years later the figure had doubled to 20,852 and by 1926 the number of people in the town had reached 102,196. Today the borough figure is in excess of 266,100, all within an area of 41 square miles.

Doubtless, Walsall was an early royal manor, the first Grant being made by Henry II to Herbert Ruffus in 1159. Associated with the Manor of Walsall in the mid-15th century was Richard Neville, Earl of Warwick, known as "the king-maker", whose crest the borough bears to this day, namely the Bear and Ragged Staff. Legend has it that Queen Elizabeth I, at some time during her reign (1558-1603), rested at the White Hart Inn on Caldmore Green and a later Queen, Henrietta Maria, wife of Charles I, also spent time in Walsall in July 1643. George Howe, playing host to her, obviously met with disapproval for he was fined £212, an enormous sum at that time!

The first mention of a Mayor of Walsall is in 1377 and during the reign of Henry IV the town became a Municipal Borough. Parliamentary Borough status followed in 1832 and on 15th October 1875 the Mayor was presented with a gold Chain of Office.

A private company converted a flooded quarry area near Lichfield Road into a pleasure garden, but it failed as a going concern, so the Council took over the freehold in 1871 and opened the place as a public park after upgrading and extending it. The Arboretum, as we now know it, covers about 80 acres and each year the Illuminations there are a great attraction.

Although subject to much architechural change, there is still a lot of the old Walsall left to see and we would invite the resident and visitor alike to look above street level and to take in the beauty of the upper storeys where the efforts and successes of earlier designers are there to be admired. And for a colourful morning out, why not join the jostling, eager bargain-hunters who descend on the outdoor market in the traffic-free High Street on market days; or, further up the street, visit the Guildhall, a once dilapidated building of Italianate design, now rescued and restored to house delightful arcades of small shops and boutiques.

For many years flooding after rain or thaw brought the town to a standstill but happily the civil engineers now appear to have solved the problem.

Town gas was first supplied to the locality when the gas-works were erected in Persehouse Street, near to the present Arboretum, in 1826, at a cost of £4,000. Subsequent moves were to sites in Wolverhampton Street and in Pleck.

Electricity supply by the Corporation began in 1895, the original generating station being in Wolverhampton Street. A move to a substantial station at Birchills came on 31st October 1916.

A Free Library was established in 1859 when Walsall became only the third town in the kingdom to adopt the Act of that year. A building was erected in Goodall Street in 1872 and enlarged in 1887. A fine new building followed in Lichfield Street in 1906, due in great part to a gift of £8,000 from the philanthropist, Andrew Carnegie.

The Arms of The Metropolitan Borough of Walsall

BEGINNINGS

By Letters Patent of 2nd July 1554, Queen Mary I gave Royal assent to the founding of a Grammar School in Walsall "for the erudition and instruction of boys and youths". Control was placed in the hands of Governors, ten men of "the more discreet and honest inhabitants of the Town and Parish of Walsall". The original school was in Church Hill, providing for 66 boys; its present site is in Sutton Road. In September 1893, a High School for Girls was opened in connection with the Grammar School and stands now in Upper Forster Street. The first Blue Coat School was held in a room over the old Market Cross at the top of High Street. A move was made in 1800 before occupation of a new site on The Bridge. Further buildings formed the school in St. Paul's Close (1859) before a final move in 1933 to new premises in Springfield Road.

Blue Coat School, St Paul's Street, The Bridge, 1921. (Now the site of the bus station).

St Bartholomew's School, Church Hill, Wednesbury, 1922.

For some children in the town today, education can start as early as two years old, whilst 80% of three year olds can obtain nursery school places. Eight special nursery schools offer part-time places to 800 pupils in addition to the 78 primary schools which provide nearly 3,000 part-time places. There are now 115 primary schools (with 25,000 pupils) and 20 comprehensives in addition to the two grammar schools. To give some idea of the wide choice of subjects available in Walsall's schools, the Sneyd Community School, in Bloxwich, even offers boating courses on its own lake.

Leamore Infants School, c. 1928.

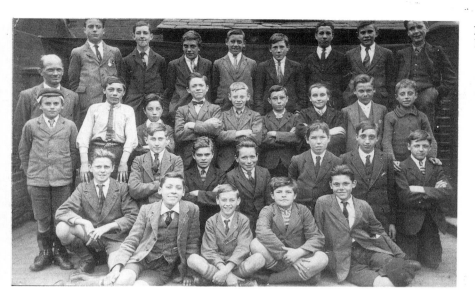

Hillary Street School, Palfrey, Walsall, c. 1929.

Blakenall Heath Junior School, Leamore, c. 1930.

NEW SCHOOLS AT WALSALL
11 MAY 1946
SWEEPING CHANGES PROPOSED

A survey of present arrangements and suggestions for future planning has been prepared by the Walsall Education Committee, to be submitted to the Minister of Education. Sweeping changes are to be made in the borough if the recommendations go through.

Suggestions are that two new Grammar Schools be established: a new Commercial High School (mixed), a new Technical High School (boys), new modern schools for secondary education in the north of the borough, the existing North Walsall (boys) and Croft Street (girls) school to be replaced by two new schools to be built on the Forest site; and Wolverhampton Road senior boys' and senior girls' schools to be replaced by two new schools.

With regard to junior schools, the report states that a considerable amount of remodelling of existing school accommodation is needed to bring it up to the standard set out in the building regulations.

The siting of schools must be closely associated with housing developments, the report adds.

The project is estimated to cost £2,000,000.

Junior Dept., Municipal School of Art, 1937.

ELMORE GREEN HIGH SCHOOL.
BLOXWICH 1947

DAY TO BE REMEMBERED AT WALSALL

POST ———————— 4 AUG 1953

Opening of Children's Lido

Records for attendance, gate receipts, and entrants in all sections marked the opening of Walsall's two-day annual horticultural show and fete in Walsall Arboretum extension yesterday. Probably the most welcome of all the records, however, was the weather, for this was the first occasion in 13 years that rain did not mar the event.

The number of people paying for admission was 30,780, compared with the previous record figure of 28,000 in 1948, and gate receipts were £2,489, against the previous highest of £1,850.

It was all the more appropriate that the weather should have been so kind on this day for it saw the opening of the first instalment of the children's lido, towards which the funds of the event have been devoted in post-war years.

If there was ever any question as to whether the lido was needed or not it was answered within seconds of Belita, the ice skating artist, officially opening the two children's paddling pools. Hardly had the tapes been cut than hundreds of children rushed for the pools and stayed there until near closing time.

Alumwell County Primary School, 27th October 1954.

Lane Head School, Short Heath, 25th April 1956.

Walsall Schools' Holiday Camp, Streetly, 30th April 1958.

Sunday School Anniversary, Salvation Army Hall, Green Lane, c. 1958.

Queen Mary's Grammar School, 16th September 1959.

A Victorian day for the pupils of Park Hall Infants School, 19th July 1979.

Members of the cast of "Oliver" from Cooper and Jordan Primary School, Aldridge, manage to get a second helping after all! 24th April 1978.

THEY ALSO SERVE

The Police were first established in the town on 6th July 1832 in good time, as it happens, for the first Parliamentary election of 13th December that year when "grave riots, confusion and destruction of property took place". By 1888 the Force had a strength of 58, costing £4,596 for the year. The expenditure on policing in 1927 was £34,856 when on strength were a Chief Constable, a Chief Inspector, 5 Inspectors, 10 Sergeants and 84 Constables.

Closely co-operating with the police, the Fire Brigade in 1905 was composed of one Superintendent and 14 men, all members of the Police Force and costing in one year £473.

Within this chapter we cannot fail to mention Sister Dora, born Dorothy Wyndlow Pattison on 15th January 1832 in Hauxwell, Yorks. She arrived in Walsall on 8th January 1865 to take charge of the Cottage Hospital, a small house in Bridge Street, which had only eight beds. During the serious smallpox outbreak in the town in 1875, sufferers refused to enter the isolation hospital until Sister Dora volunteered to take charge and to nurse them. For six months she lived at the hospital alone except for her patients. Her work in the town's hospitals continued tirelessly and cheerfully until by 4th November 1878 she was very ill and obviously dying and the Mayor had to deputise for her in opening the new hospital that she had pioneered. On a gloomy, foggy Christmas Eve, 1878, she died and the whole town went into mourning for her. A statue in her memory was unveiled on The Bridge on 11th October 1886 and it was said at the time to be the first statue in England to be erected in memory of an uncrowned lady.

Staff, St John's School, Russell Street, Wednesbury, 1916.

Departure of the 5th Battalion, South Staffs Regiment for The Western Front, 11th August 1914. On the back of the card Pollie has written "Isn't the war terrible?".

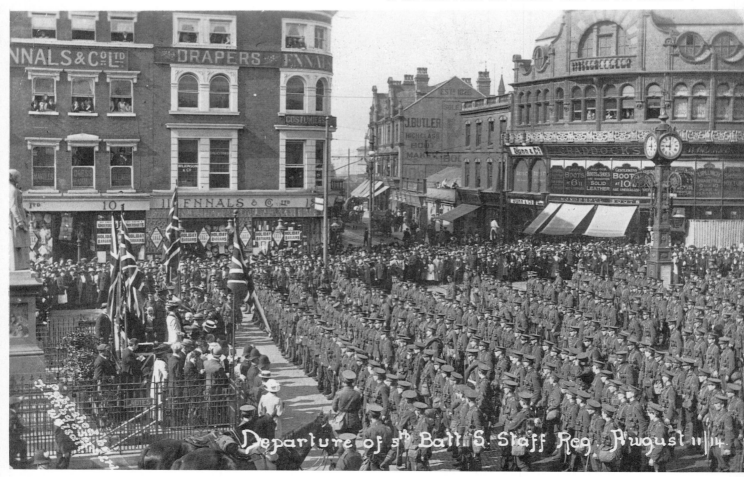

No. 16 Platoon, 32nd Battalion (South Staffs.) Home Guard, Helliwells Ltd., Walsall Airport, 1944.

ARP (Air Raid Precautions) Wardens' Choir, with their guest vocalist Doris Attwood, c. 1940.

Group, Civil Defence Wardens, Darlaston, c. 1943.

Long service medals are presented to Brownhills and Chasetown Special Constables by Coun. Breeze, Chairman of Brownhills Urban District Council, September 1950.

Police inspection, the Town Hall, 14th April 1931.

Walsall Fire Brigade, The Grange, 1941.

National Fire Service Water Unit, The Grange, 1943. The large van carried reeled hoses which, when coupled, could draw on long distance water supplies.

RECENT FLARE-UPS IN WALSALL. SEPT 1892

Last month holds the record for the greatest number of fires in Walsall. The majority of them were small and happily resulted in little loss and very slight inconvenience. Of the whole number those which occurred on the premises of Mr. R. E. Thacker, saddlers' ironmonger and manufacturer, and Mr. J. Carver, whip manufacturer, were the most serious. The damage in both cases was great, and, although both were covered by insurance, the inconvenience caused for the time was, to say the least, undesirable. Mr. Thacker's fire occurred at midnight on Thursday, the 11th ult. It appears to have first broken out in or above the casting shop, through, it is thought, the over-heating of the flue. The Fire Brigade was soon in attendance, and succeeded in subduing the flames, with the loss of only one block of shopping—the one in which the casting, plating, and finishing were carried on. Luckily, it was a calm night. Had there been anything like a strong wind blowing nothing could possibly have saved the whole factory. The damage is estimated at about £800, including building and stock. Fortunately for Mr. Thacker, on the opposite side of the road was an empty block of shopping just suited for the purpose of casting, silver-plating, and finishing, which he at once secured, where he placed his workpeople, who proceeded with their work with little interruption. Mr. Thacker had on hand a large stock of goods, so that customers at a distance would not have noticed that anything unusual had occurred, and by the time this appears in print the whole concern will be in full swing, with the exception of a little extra running about for the warehousemen and clerks.

A week later, in the dinner hour, the recently-erected and roomy factory of Mr. J. Carver was found to be in flames, and so fierce was the conflagration that before two o'clock the roof had fallen in. The fire seems to have first arisen on the top storey, where Mr. Carver had stored a great deal of inflammable material, including a small portion of his holly sticks. These, of course, needed no second invitation to catch on the spirit of the hour. Mr. Carver's factory is situate on fairly high ground, and on this account the Fire Brigade was unable for a time to get a sufficient force of water to cope with the flames; but when more pressure was put on the mains, the fire was soon got under. The damage here is estimated at between £4,000 and £5,000. Mr. Carver had recently put down a large plant of new machinery, which, however, escaped much damage.

13

Nurses, firemen and St John Ambulance personnel,
Rubery Owen & Co. Ltd., 1943.

Manor Hospital, Walsall, 1949.

Hospital Management Committee—Back Row : Mr. C. W. Eynon, Dr. R. H. M. Baines, B.M., B.Ch. Mr. H. J. Grubb, (Deputy Group Secretary), Mr. A. Anderton, A.H.A. (Finance Officer). Second Row : Mr. Robert Forrest, M.B., Ch.B., Mr. H. J. Hunter, J.P., Councillor Mrs. M. M. Owen, Mr. J. S. Minton, J.P., Dr. T. Ross, M.B., Ch.B., D.P.H., Miss K. M. Orgill, Mr. A. Lucas, J.P. Front Row : Mr. Gilbert Harvey, Mrs. G. M. Tomkinson, J.P., Mr. J. N. F. Cotterell, M.B.E., J.P. (Vice-Chairman), Mr. H. W. Bonner, J.P. (Chairman), Mr. H. Woodhead, J.P., Mrs. P. M. Eglington, M.B.E., Mr. J. L. Weston, M.B., Ch.B.
1963

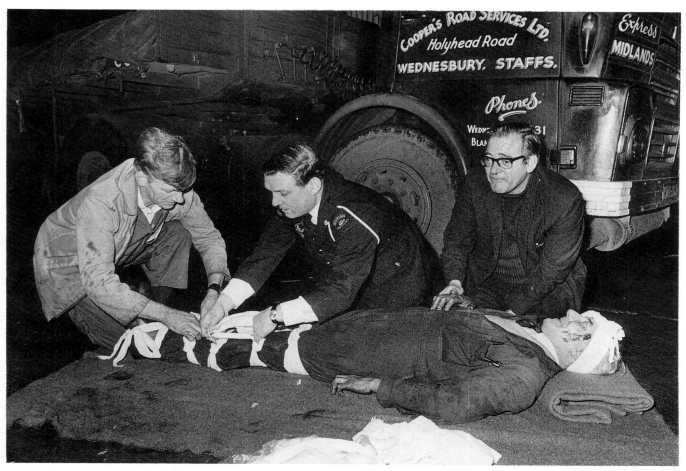

A mock-up accident is just part of the Red Cross training, 29th November 1972.

St John Ambulance members parade at Walsall Football Ground, 18th April 1966.

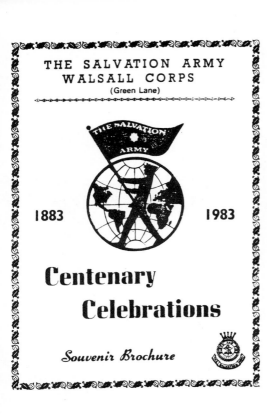

THE SALVATION ARMY
WALSALL CORPS
(Green Lane)

1883   1983

Centenary
Celebrations

Souvenir Brochure

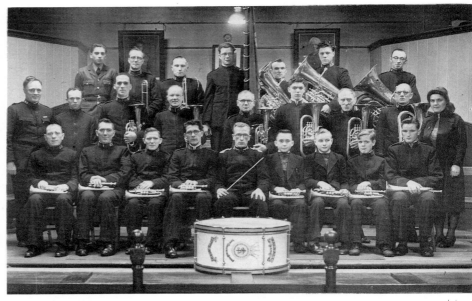

Salvation Army Band, c. 1946.

Demonstration of outdoor cookery by WVS (now WRVS) members, Brownhills, 1943.

Aldridge UDC (Urban District Council), 1934.

Willenhall UDC, c. 1948.

Coun. Wadsworth introduces a deputation to the Council Meeting at Tynings Lane School, Aldridge, during the Annual General Meeting, 31st May 1961.

Youth Week Parade,
15th May 1959.

18

EVENTS

The foundation stone of the new Council House in Lichfield Street was laid by Prince Christian, brother-in-law of King Edward VII, on 29th May 1902 and the official opening of the completed building was in 1905. Edward, Prince of Wales, later to become Edward VIII, visited the town in the course of his tour of South Staffordshire in June 1923. Princess Arthur of Connaught came to open the Hospital Bazaar in November 1926.

Britain's first Mighty Wurlitzer Orchestra Organ, having two manuals, was installed in the Picture House, Bridge Street, in January 1925. Although it was removed in 1955 it is still in use in a church at Beer, South Devon.

Jerome K. Jerome, the world-famous author and dramatist was born in Belsize House, on the corner of Caldmore Road and Bradford Street on 2nd May 1859. His success was recognised when he was admitted to be an Honorary Freeman of the Borough on 10th November 1926. This was conferred on him on 17th February 1927 but sadly he lived only for a few months after this event. Belsize House was opened as his museum in 1984.

Although in use some years earlier, Walsall Airport was officially opened on 6th July 1935. The airfield licence was finally rescinded in 1958.

The Saddler Centre, between Park Street and Bradford Street, came into public use on 24th March 1980 and was officially opened by Sir Peter Parker on 18th July 1980. The centre is now visited by more than 165,000 shoppers each week. The railway station within the complex and the close proximity of the bus stations give ideal service to visitors to the centre which is now known as just the Saddlers.

alsall Photographic Society, on a visit to Patshull Park, ar Wolverhampton, c. 1896.

e Woodman Inn, Wood Green, Wednesbury, c. 1900. this a trip? A club outing? Was the man with the adstone bag a doctor or the treasurer?

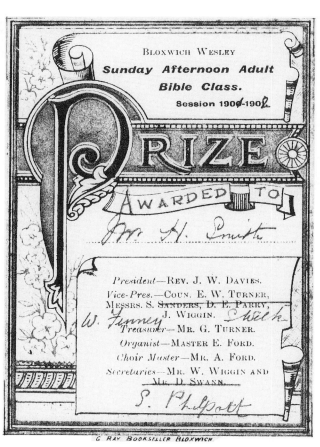

The wedding of Mr and Mrs Noah Granger, Wednesbury Church, 1906.

Crabtrees' staff outing, 1923.

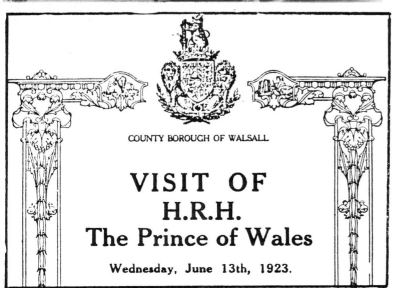

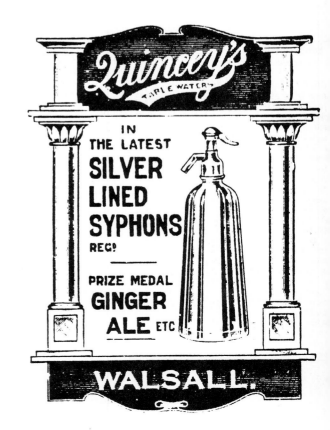

20

Opening of the new Willenhall Drill Hall, 22nd March 1924.

Amy Johnson, the famous flying ace, visits Walsall Airport, 1930.

Leamore Wesley Church Bazaar, 1936.

The Silver Jubilee Celebrations,

— MONDAY, 6TH MAY, 1935. —

BLOXWICH :: STAFFORD :: ROAD
SPORTS' :: CLUB.

ANGLO-AMERICAN WEEK FEB 1945

WALSALL TRIBUTE TO U.S. FORCES

To Walsall has fallen the distinction of having the first Anglo-American Week to be held in this country. Arranged primarily to enable the town to express its appreciation of the help received in regard to many war efforts from the American Forces, it will be used also to foster Anglo-American relations.

From February 19 to February 24 there will be a comprehensive programme of entertainments, exhibitions of American equipment, visits to factories, schools and clubs by parties of American soldiers, addresses on Anglo-American relations by Professor Newell, and many other events.

The Hospitality Committee is arranging for a number of American soldiers to be received as guests in Walsall homes.

The week will conclude on Saturday, February 24, with a presentation by the Mayor (Councillor John Whiston) of a Standard to the American Forces, about 1,000 of whom will attend a parade in The Arboretum and afterwards march through the town.

THURSDAY, 22nd, FEBRUARY, 1945.

10 a.m. till dusk.
Municipal Car Park, Lichfield Street. American Forces Motorised Exhibition.

11 a.m. — 6-30 p.m.
Lecture Hall, Town Hall, (Leicester Street Entrance.) American Forces Exhibition.

7 p.m. — 11-30 p.m.
Town Hall, (Leicester Street Entrance.) Grand Anglo-American Dance.

American " Stars of Swing " Band
Of the U.S.A. 10th. Replacement Depot, Leader: Corpl. Tony Spair, (By kind permission of Officer Commanding.)

British Dance Rythm
By the Dance Orchestra of the 1st. Battalion The South Staffs. Regiment. Leader: Bandmaster H. H. Thatcher, (by kind permission of Major D. Stevens, M.M.)

Grand All American " Jitterbug " Competition
M.C.'s and Judges:— Corporal Billy Taft and Corporal Eugene Cohen. (Stars of " Lets' Be Buddies.")

7 p.m.
Tower Street Swimming Baths.

Anglo-American Aquatic Gala
Events by Sea Cadets, Army Cadet Force & Air Training Corps
(By kind permission of their respective Commanding Officers).
Diving Display by Sgt. Richard Gurney, Sectional Diving Champion, U.S. Army, Jefferson, Iowa.
Diving Display by the School Children of Walsall.

Grand Swimming Display:—

Representing England	Miss Edna Hughes, English 100 yards Champion and Olympic Games Representative from 1932 to 1938.
Representing America.	Cpl. William Gushue, District Champion of Eastern Counties, Buffalo, New York State. Has represented Eastern States against Canada, South America and the American Home States. Captain Gordon, Dedham, Mass., Sgt. Richard Gurney, Council Bluff, Iowa., Sgt. Robert Fitzgerald, Los Angeles, Calf. Sgt. Bernard Levine, Brooklyn, N.Y., Sgt. Mike Kozo, New Brunswick, New Jersey. Pvt. J. Leckliter, Philadelphia, Pa., Pvt. Stanley Oaker, Pittsburg, Pa., Cpl. William Gushue, Buffalo, N.Y.

Future of Germany

WHAT is to be done with Germany. As a nation she ought to revert to the status of a third-rate Power in Europe. Until 1866 Germany was but a number of small states, and Prussia a separate kingdom which was annexed to Germany, and became absorbed into the German Empire.

Let her shrink territorially that it may be impossible for ever to become a power again in Europe. Now that she is beaten a second time in the bid for world domination and conquest, and brought to her knees, let her be kept down under the iron heel of the Allied Nations. O. SWANN. Walsall. 10.5.45

WILL OF MR. PAT COLLINS

Showman King Leaves £72,419

Mr. Pat Collins, of Lime Tree House, Bloxwich, Walsall, amusement caterer, president of the Showmen's Guild of Great Britain for 20 years, Liberal M.P. for Walsall from 1922-24, who died on December 8th last, aged 83 years, left £72,419 4s. gross, with net personalty £12,625.

Probate has been granted to his widow, and to John N. F. Cotterell, solicitor, of Bridge Street, Walsall, to Harry Coad, of 34 Vincent Street, Walsall, and James B. Cooper, of Rowley Street, Walsall. *1944*

BOTHER OVER A BOARD

THERE'S a bother in Walsall about a second-hand pastry board. Such a bother, that £2 is offered for its safe delivery to a local dealer's yard at 50a, Corporation-street.

All because of this pastry board two merchants are at loggerheads. One bought it, missed it, and thought it got into the other's lot by mistake.

It didn't.

Unlooked for, probably unwanted, the pastry board is worth only two shillings, wherever it was sent after a sale at Broadway North, Walsall.

But it is worth 20 times its kitchen value to the disputing dealers. *24.2.50*

HANDBAG FOR PRINCESS

19 APR 1951

Gift Planned by Council

PRESENTATION ON MAY 1

When Princess Margaret visits Walsall on May 1 she will probably be presented with a semi-chrome gold-coloured crocodile Walsall handbag, costing about £30, by the Corporation.

A sample of the bag—plain tailored type—is at present being made at the Walsall leather firm of Wilmot Bennett, of Midland Road, where a foreman, Mr. G. A. Fletcher, of 29, Bernard Street, Walsall, has the responsible task of supervising the design.

Leather Handle

The finished bag will not be of the shoulder-strap type, but will have a leather handle.

The inside will be lined with beige-coloured suede and fitted with a crocodile purse, divided pockets and a mirror.

The frame of the bag is being made by Broadhurst and Thompson Ltd., of 35, Birmingham Street, Walsall.

Princess Margaret inspects the Guard of Honour, Park Street, 1st May 1951.

23

Senior Citizens' Christmas Party, Leys Hall, Darlaston, 1952.

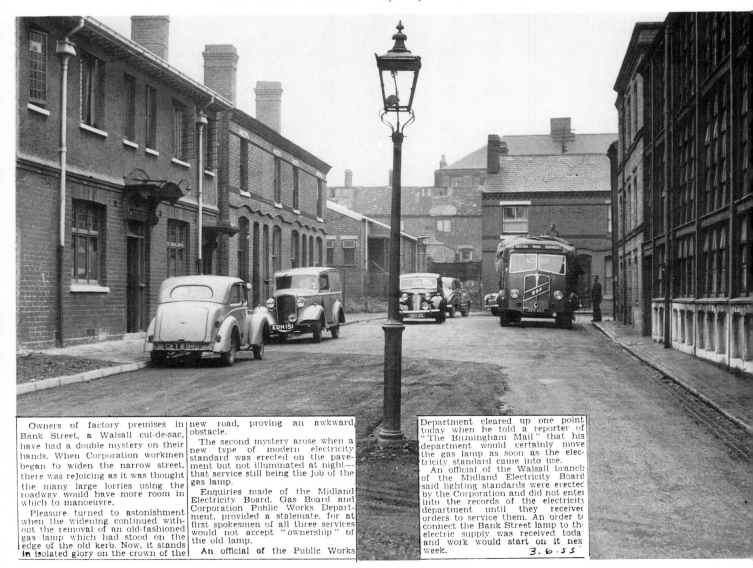

Owners of factory premises in Bank Street, a Walsall cul-de-sac, have had a double mystery on their hands. When Corporation workmen began to widen the narrow street, there was rejoicing as it was thought the many large lorries using the roadway would have more room in which to manoeuvre.

Pleasure turned to astonishment when the widening continued without the removal of an old-fashioned gas lamp which had stood on the edge of the old kerb. Now, it stands in isolated glory on the crown of the new road, proving an awkward obstacle.

The second mystery arose when a new type of modern electricity standard was erected on the pavement but not illuminated at night—that service still being the job of the gas lamp.

Enquiries made of the Midland Electricity Board, Gas Board and Corporation Public Works Department, provided a stalemate, for at first spokesmen of all three services would not accept "ownership" of the old lamp.

An official of the Public Works Department cleared up one point today when he told a reporter of "The Birmingham Mail" that his department would certainly move the gas lamp as soon as the electricity standard came into use.

An official of the Walsall branch of the Midland Electricity Board said lighting standards were erected by the Corporation and did not enter into the records of the electricity department until they received orders to service them. An order to connect the Bank Street lamp to the electric supply was received today and work would start on it next week. 3. 6. 55

24

SISTER DORA STATUE TO BE UNVEILED THIS MONTH

Walsall's new bronze statue to commemorate the memory of Sister Dora Pattison, the town's nursing pioneer, will be unveiled by Coun. H. S. Gwinnutt on January 16, when the annual birthday celebrations take place.

Although the statue has been on its pedestal in the centre of the town for many months, it has remained hidden from view under a shroud of waterproof wrappings.

The original Sister Dora statue, also provided by public subscription, was the first memorial to be erected in the country to a woman outside royalty.

Corrosion

In recent years the marble corroded badly, and in 1954-55 the then Mayor, Coun. Gwinnutt, appealed for money to provide a replacement. More than £1,400 was raised. Then it was discovered that the panels depicting scenes of Sister Dora's devotion to duty had also deteriorated, and the corporation decided to have bronze casts made at a further cost of £1,000. 2.1.57

Battle of Britain Parade, High Street, 18th September 1955.

Mail 1.10.58

PREMIER MEETS THE MIDLAND HERCULES

"Mail" Staff Reporter

MR. Macmillan saw the strong men of Midland industry at work today—the chain-makers of the Black Country.

The Prime Minister's visit to the Walsall chain-making firm of Wheways Ltd., was the highlight of the second full day of his "meet the people" tour of the Midlands.

He saw the old and the new in chain-making technique.

The old was demonstrated for him at an open forge by 59-year-old Mr. Edwin Barnett, whose father and grandfather before him worked at this traditional Black Country trade.

The new was demonstrated for him in the modern welding and bending shops.

"Ah," said Mr. Macmillan, "This takes the backache out of the job, doesn't it?"

ANOTHER DIVERSION

The Prime Minister, who was given a typical Black Country welcome by a big crowd outside the works, was taken on his tour of the factory by Mr. Robert Wheway, who represents the fourth generation in this family concern.

Labour Party leader Hugh Gaitskell addresses the Midland Area Miners' Gala at the Arboretum, 27th June 1959.

Laying the foundation stone at the Tower Street Baths, 22nd July 1960.

Unveiling the statue outside the Technical College, 23rd September 1960.

Princess Alexandra at the official opening of the McKechnie Metal's site, Middlemore Lane, Aldridge, 5th May 1961.

St George's Day Parade, Willenhall, 5th May 1962.

Celebrating the Queen's visit, 24th May 1962.

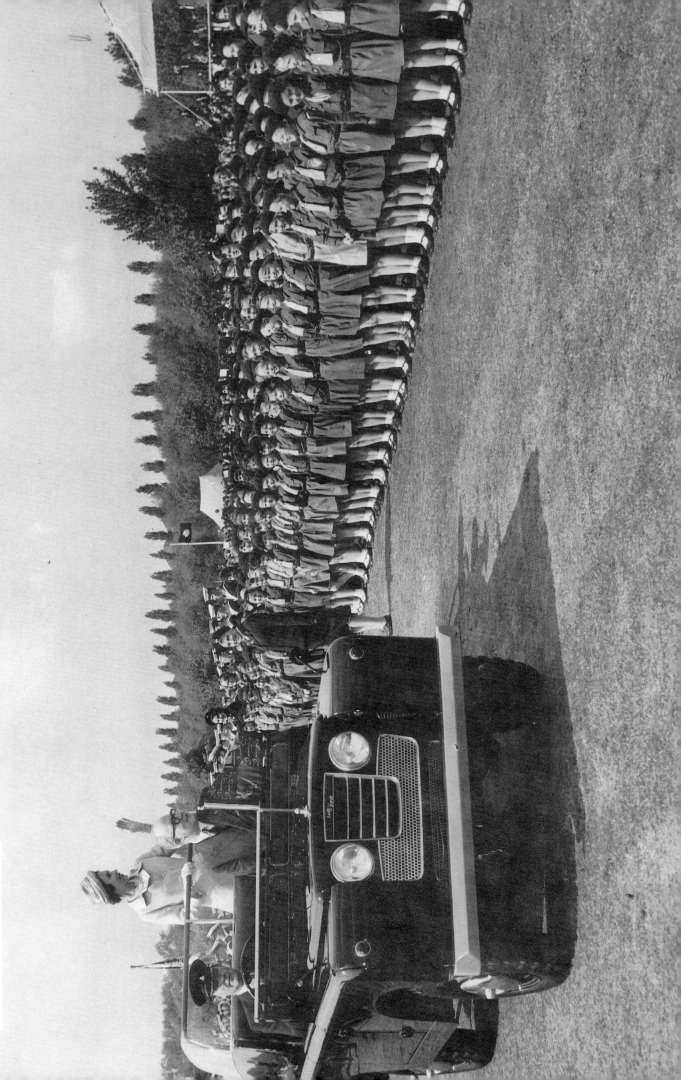

The Queen visits the Arboretum, 24th May 1962.

The opening ceremony at the Paddock multi-storey flats, 7th November 1969.

Wellman Smith Owen Engineering Corp. Ltd. 1964

DARLASTON employees, their wives and families will be off at Whitsun on the 17th annual works outing.

It is anticipated that 300 will be boarding the "WSO Special" on Saturday, June 5th for the journey to Blackpool and a four-day stay at Pontin's Holiday Camp.

The outing, which is organised by the Fitting Shop, was first held back in 1947.

The event is linked to the Darlaston shilling-a-week football sweep, the pool being shared out before the Whitsun trip.

Many have more than one share, however, and use the fund as a savings bank.

Employees who do not go on the outing get back half of what they have paid in during the season.

Fitting Shop foreman **Mr Ernie Ramsbottom** is chairman of the Fund and he remembers some of the highlights of the past.

One such occasion was an outing to Middleton Towers which is recalled in our photograph – of Darlaston employees on holiday and of the train which took them there.

"We had 550 go one year," says Mr Ramsbottom, "and had to have TWO special trains to take us. You need 300 for a special and we've attained that on all but two occasions."

British Red Cross annual inspection, Upper Rushall Street, 1975.

What an end to the year! A submerged car is recovered from the floods in Bridgeman Street, 30th December 1978.

Contestants for the title "Miss Coronation 1983", promoted by the Coronation pub, Friar Park Road, Wednesbury, 15th September 1983.

Princess Diana visits the Dr Barnardo's Centre, Walsall Wood Road, Aldridge, on a very cold day, 19th February 1986.

Prince Charles talks to the people of Walsall outside the Guildhall, 26th November 1987.

Princess Anne opens the Walsall Leather Museum, Wisemore, 10th June 1988.

WALSALL LEATHER CENTRE

ON THE MOVE

The first Turnpike Act relating to Walsall was passed in 1748, prior to which the town lay completely out of the line of general traffic, due almost entirely to the "narrow, tortuous, ruinous and dangerous condition of the roads". Traffic to and from Birmingham had to pass down High Street, Ablewell Street was not even a carriage-way and Bridge Street did not exist at all. An Act of 1771 ordered Bridge Street to be constructed. However, improvements under an Act of 1793 made the old routes obsolete and the whole of the Birmingham traffic began to flow through the town.

On 4th July 1837 the Grand Junction Railway was formally opened with a small station at Bescot Bridge for the convenience of Walsall people who were then conveyed to and from the George Hotel by other means. During 1846 the South Staffordshire Railway was constructed, giving a direct line from Dudley through Bescot and Walsall to Rushall. Ten years later the Wolverhampton line was in operation. Eventually the LMS (London, Midland & Scottish) Railway was serving the borough although the GWR (Great Western Railway) had to seek certain powers to run within the same area.

The Walsall Corporation Acts of 1914, 1919, 1935 and later gave wide powers to run motor buses in and around the Borough.

An advertisement of 4th November 1754 states: "The Stage Coach will call at the Three Swans in Walsall; Fare to London — £1. 4s. 0d. (£1.20)". The journey, 120 miles, took three whole days and that was considered a good time then. Compare that with the record sea-plane flight by Walsall's own Flt. Lieut. S.N. Webster, RAF, on 26th September 1927 when he captured the Schneider Trophy for Britain in the greatest air-race in the world at that time. He covered the course of 217 miles at the Lido, Venice, at an average speed of 281.40 miles per hour.

A leisurely trip down the canal, c. 1895.

The last steam tram at King's Hill, Wednesbury, 15th
June 1904.

Looking towards Pleck from the foot of Wednesbury
Road railway bridge, 1913.

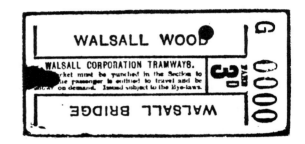

WALSALL WOOD
WALSALL CORPORATION TRAMWAYS.
WALSALL BRIDGE

THE LAST TRAMCAR.

30.9.33

End of Rail-Track System Which Walsall Has Had for Nearly Fifty Years.

BLOXWICH TROLLEY-BUSES TO-MORROW.

Tramcars, steam or electric, have been running in Walsall for nearly fifty years (the first steam service was inaugurated in December, 1884); but in recent years petrol omnibuses have been steadily ousting them, until the only route on which they have remained for the past four and a half years has been that between The Bridge and Bloxwich.

Now they have come to the end of their service, for to-night's last car is the last that will run on a rail track in Walsall. To-morrow (Sunday) they will be superseded by electric trolley 'buses.

COUNTY BOROUGH OF WALSALL.

1935

TRANSPORT DEPARTMENT.

A FREQUENT Service of Trolley Vehicles or Motor Omnibuses operate from the centre of the Town to all parts of the Borough and the whole of the surrounding districts. These services are inter-connected with other road passenger transport systems, thus giving adequate travelling facilities to the whole of the Midlands.

ROUTES.

Walsall-Cannock-Hednesford
Bloxwich, New Invention and Willenhall
Fullbrook
. Walsall-Brownhills-Hednesford
Walsall-Chasetown-Hednesford
Walsall-Aldridge-Sutton Cold-field
Hednesford-Pye Green-Cannock
Hednesford-Cannock Wood via Rawnsley
Walsall Wood-Shenstone
. Reedswood
. Walsall-Pelsall-Brownhills
. Walsall-Chasetown-Cannock
. Walsall-Streetly
. Walsall-West Bromwich
. Walsall-Blakenall-Bloxwich
. Walsall-Lichfield
. Walsall-Norton-Cannock
. Bloxwich-Cheslyn Hay
. Walsall-Burntwood
. Cannock-Rugeley via Old Hednesford Road
. Walsall-Barr Common-Bloxwich.
. Heath Hayes-Cannock-Cheslyn Hay

23 Walsall-Walsall Wood-Brownhills
24. Paddock
25. Pleck Road
26. Birmingham Road
27. Hednesford-Cannock Wood via Hazel Slade
28. Walsall-Willenhall
29. Walsall-Wolverhampton
30. Walsall-Bloxwich
31. Bloxwich to New Invention
32. Bradford Place to Walstead Road-Delves.
33. Cannock-Wimblebury-Hednesford
34. Walsall-Leamore
35. Inner Circle.
36. Cannock-Hednesford via Huntington Terrace
37. Walsall-Wednesbury-Darlaston-Walsall
38. Walsall-Darlaston-Wednesbury-Walsall
39. Walsall-Pleck
40. Alum Well Road
41. Walsall-New Invention-Willenhall.
42 Cannock-Belt Road via Blackfords.

Full detail Time Tables on application.

Places of historic interest and famous beauty spots served by the Omnibus Services include Cannock Chase, Shoal Hill, Sutton Park, Blake Street, Barr Beacon, Lichfield, and the Roman excavations at Letocetum.

Special Omnibuses may be reserved for Private Parties.

PARCEL & MESSENGER SERVICE.

Express deliveries made Daily in all districts served by Trolley Vehicle and Motor Omnibus Services.

Messengers may be engaged for Direct Parcel Service, etc. Terms on application.

TRANSPORT DEPT. PARCEL EXPRESS ensures **QUICK DELIVERY.**

M. J. SOMERFIELD,
General Manager.

Transport Offices ('Phone 2259),
WALSALL.

Congestion on the Bridge is to be relieved by the transfer of the Bloxwich trolley bus terminus to St Paul's Street. 23rd August 1950.

Bloxwich bus terminus, near the Bull's Head, 1952.

A HUGE CLANGING OF HEARTSTRINGS

They queued with their cameras at the trolleybus stop, and queued with their letters at the library.

Walsall people certainly gave the town's trolleybus service a great send off today.

A special postmark designed for the occasion and commemorative trolley-bus trips between Walsall and Bloxwich marked the final day for the vehicle in the town.

After just an hour and a half special envelopes at the library were sold out, and only ordinary letters could be mailed bearing the commemorative postmark.

Over 1,500 envelopes had been printed for the occasion and organisers of the special post box in the library were amazed at the rush.

The library doorway was blocked most of the morning by people queueing for stamps.

Other queued for their last trolley bus run armed with cameras to record the event. 3.10.70

The last trolley bus in public service prepares to leave Walsall Bus Station for Bloxwich, 3rd October 1970.

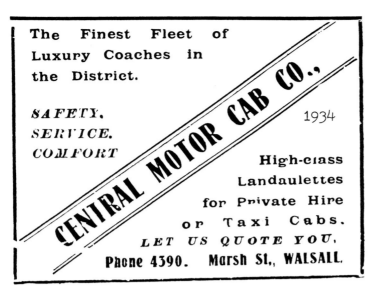

Bell Lane, Bloxwich, 6th November 1963.

Bescot sidings, 1955.

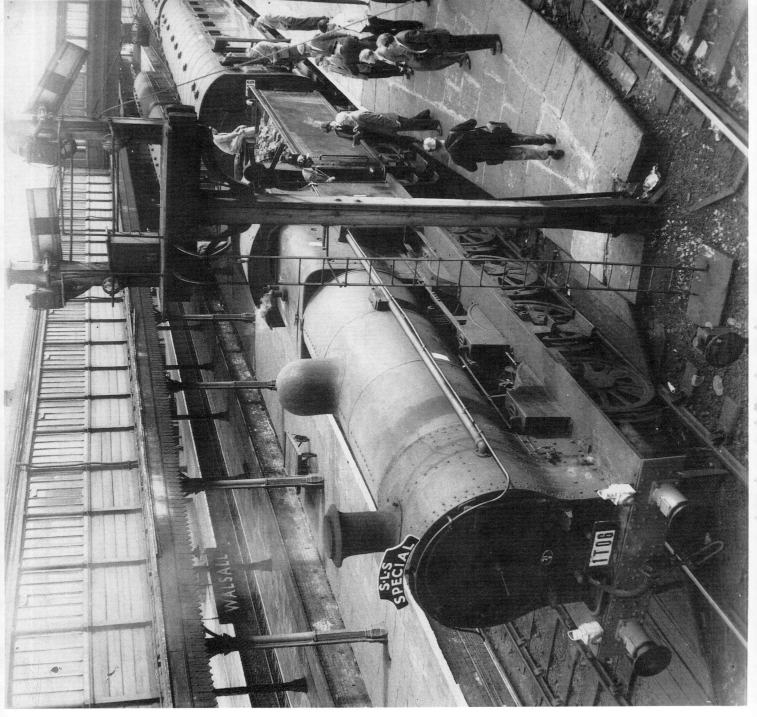

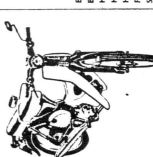

Pines Express, to Bath, changing engines, Walsall Station, 1959.

39

AT WORK

Being described as "The Town of One Hundred Trades" hardly does true justice to Walsall. Indeed, its claim to be a leader in the manufacture of saddles, harnesses and leather goods is never in dispute, for this has been the situation ever since the mid-19th century. The Leather Centre Museum in Wisemore demonstrates very well the expertise of craft-workers who display many of the skills behind traditional English leatherwork. On entering the buildings the visitor will instantly become aware of that delightful and nostalgic smell of real leather!

Before 1939, Helliwells Ltd., based at Walsall Airport on the Aldridge Road near to Longwood Bridge, were making "Swallow" side-cars for motor-cycles, and during World War II they were engaged on sub-contract work for the Air Ministry.

Crabtree Electrical Industries Ltd., Beacon Street, are makers of electrical wiring and switches on a grand scale.

Good road and rail links greatly facilitate the movement of the town's finished goods to customers at home and abroad.

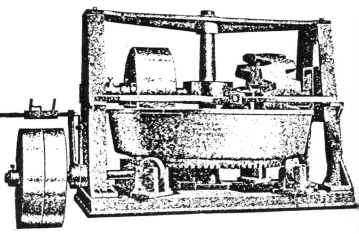

Cyclops Iron Works, Pleck Road, 1901.

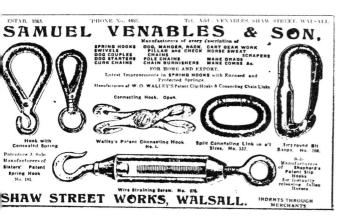
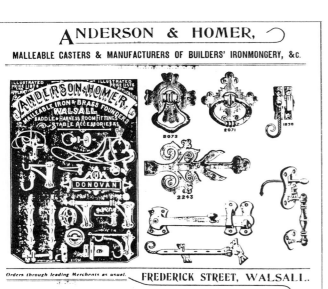
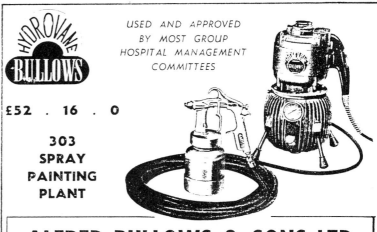

Crabtree, Upper Rushall Street, 1922.

From the crudest hulk to the last gallant ship under sail—from the very beginning of his struggle with the sea—man has been forced to accept a varying degree of personal discomfort as an inevitable condition of ocean travel.

Yet we take the palatial comfort of the "Queen Mary" for granted and pass from one continent to another in a modern city afloat.

To pause and reflect, is to realise that this tremendous development has been made almost within living memory.

Such progress is of our time. It drives us on at so relentless a rate that we are tempted to peer anxiously ahead. We should be in no doubt. Our privilege is to live in these days. Our task is to pioneer the new age a-dawning.

CRABTREE

A name synonymous with Progress in Accessories and Switchgear

DIAMOND CRABTREE JUBILEE

1919 1979

WOMEN OF BRITAIN
COME INTO THE FACTORIES
ASK AT ANY EMPLOYMENT EXCHANGE FOR ADVICE AND FULL DETAILS

Dept. 19, Rubery Owen & Co. Ltd., Darlaston, 2nd July 1941.

McKechnie Bros., Aldridge, 19th March 1958.

Laying the foundations for the office block, McKechnie Bros., 27th May 1958.

Princess Margaret at Rubery Owen, 21st November 1962.

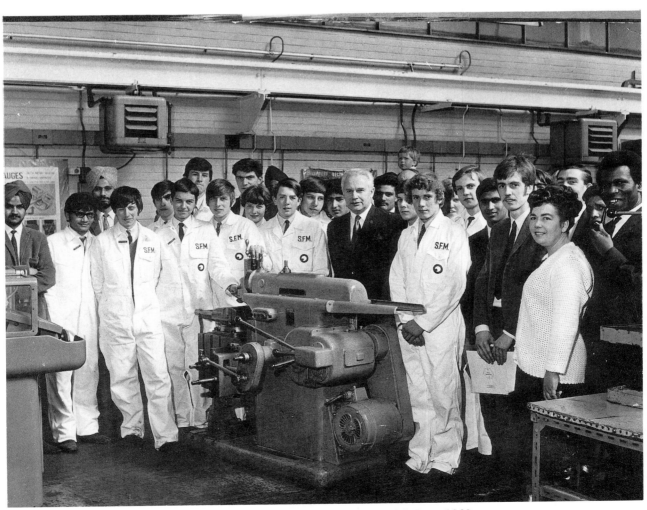

S.F. Mokes Ltd., Rollingmill Street, 13th June 1969.

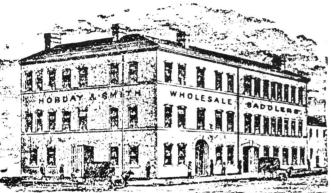

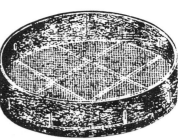
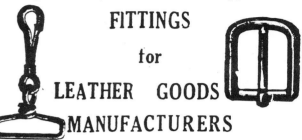

Coal jagging (the selling of small loads of coal) in Russell Street, by William Potter of Holloway Bank, Wednesbury, 1908.

Broadway/Birmingham Road, 8th December 1954.

Barbara and David Lewis relaunched the Walsall Hame and Cart Gear Company in 1986. The company was the last surviving hand forger of shire horse hames (the curved bars attached to a draught horse collar).

A hand-sewn football, made by Jabez Cliff and Co. Ltd.,
Lower Forster Street.

D. Power and Sons (glove manufacturers), Long Str
c. 1933.

Walsall Corporation Tramways Staff and Committee, c. 1926.

Walsall Tram Depot, 1927.

E. Tomkins' Coach and Taxi Office, Hatherton Street, 6th September 1934. General Booth (Founder of The Salvation Army) stayed in this house during his 1866 campaign.

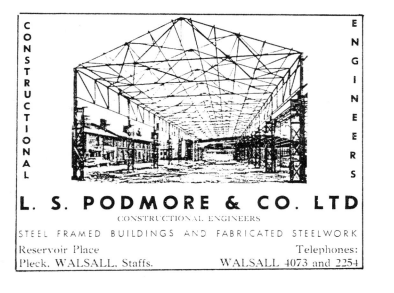
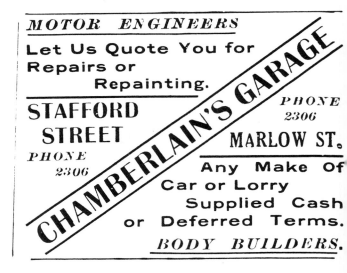

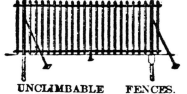

Repairs to Townend, 23rd November 1954.

51

Laying the main northern sewer,
High Street, Bloxwich, 1st April 1957.

The new Town Hall floor takes shape, 7th March 1955.

53

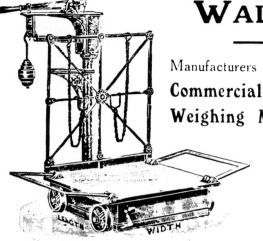

54

Walsall Market, 1st May 1971.

Shopping Week Exhibition, Town Hall, 1931. Garnett Orton's shop was in Park Street.

Aldridge Careers Exhibition, Walsall Airport, 30th April 1958.

The original Observer Office, Bridge Street, c. 1880.

South Staffs. Aero Club, The Aerodrome, Aldridge Road, Walsall.—Chief Instrs.: C. M. D. Chambers, Mgr. J. J. Wilson. Hon. Sec.: E. Turley. Machines maintained by Airports Ltd.
Fees: (flying) no entrance, annual sub. £2 2s., (non-flying) annual sub. 10s. 6d. Rates: dual £2. solo £1 7s. 6d. and special contract rates for complete courses.
Fleet: Tiger Moth and Gipsy Moth.
Aerodrome on edge of Black Country. Immediately to North and East is open country ideal for cross-country flying. **8339**

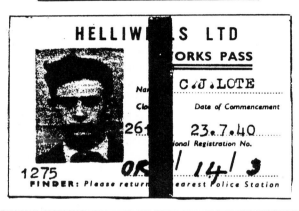

HELLIWELLS LTD
WORKS PASS
Name C.J.LOTE
Clo... 26...
Date of Commencement
23.7.40
National Registration No.
ORN/14/3
1275
FINDER: Please return nearest Police Station

Helliwell's Ltd., Walsall Airport, 1948.

Elmore Green High School F.C., Bloxwich, 1946/7.

AT PLAY

It is certain that whenever Walsall Football Club is mentioned someone will recall that wonderful day, 14th January 1933, when our local Third Division (North) team, of no particular skills, took on Arsenal, then the most powerful team in the country, and beat them 2-0, thus knocking them out of the F.A. Cup. They won on merit and Gilbert Alsop, the centre-forward, always a local hero, scored one of the goals. Formed in 1888 by the amalgamation of two Walsall teams, the Swifts and the Town, Walsall F.C. presently play at Fellows Park but hope soon to move to a modern stadium near Bescot Crescent. Willenhall Town F.C. was formed as Willenhall F.C. after World War I, combining two local teams. The club folded in 1929 but was revived in 1953 as Willenhall Town F.C., again by an amalgamation, this time between Aston Road Villa and Willenhall RAFA. The team played at the Memorial Park until 1975 but then moved to its present ground in Noose Lane. Growing bands of supporters are attracted to other local teams striving to play good football.

Such is the playing strength of Walsall Rugby Football Club (with their ground in Delves Road) that they can regularly field five senior teams and one Colts' team.

In the old days Walsall was well known for its horse-races on a good course, but in 1879 the land was acquired by the Midland Railway Company, the grandstand sold and then demolished. No further race meetings were held in the town.

1833 saw the establishment of the town's Cricket Club when they leased a ground in the Chuckery before a move to their present ground off Gorway Road on 24th April 1909. Two of the famous Grace brothers had earlier visited the Chuckery ground on 20th August 1874 with an All-England XI.

The Corporation opened public baths in Tower Street in 1896 when mustard packs, Turkish baths, Russian baths, sitz, pine, brine, sulphur and foam baths were available. During the winter the swimming baths were converted to public halls for dancing and other functions. The buildings were demolished in 1959 and two years later the Gala Baths were erected on the site.

The first film with a sound-track was screened at the Picture House, Bridge Street, on 26th August 1929. There were long queues each day during that week to see (and hear) "The Singing Fool". The Talkies had arrived in Walsall! Before World War II there was a wide choice of cinemas in the town, among them the Forum (Caldmore Green), the Cinema de Luxe (Stafford Street), Her Majesty's Theatre (Park Street), the Palace (The Old Square) and the Picture House (Bridge Street). Now, sadly, just one, the Cannon, remains, although it does have three screens. It is on the site in Park Street where Her Majesty's (later the Savoy) stood.

Darlaston Town F.C., 15th December 1956.

Walsall Rugby Football Club, 4th April 1953.

61

Walsall C.C., 27th May 1950.

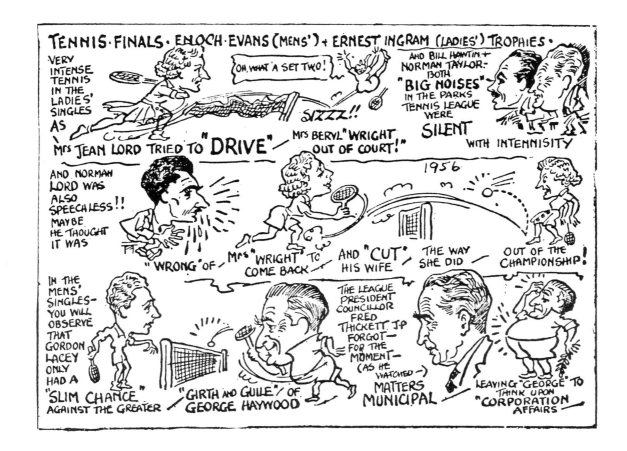

Bloxwich Golf Club, 1931.

King's Arms Bowling Club, High Street, Bloxwich, c. 1930.

Walsall MEB Netball Team, 19th July 1979.

Some of the Midland area under-16 Hockey Championship finalists at their school, Pelsall Comprehensive, 7th April 1981.

Wednesbury Primary Schools' swimming champions, 19th July 1978.

65

Walsall Polo Team, winners of the National Club Water Polo Championship, Birmingham & District Water Polo League Division One and the Stafford County Championship, 1922.

The Fire Service Benevolent Fund benefited to the sum of over £400 after eight off-duty firemen took part in a 24-hour marathon, 4th August 1982.

Park Street, with the Grand Theatre on the left and Her Majesty's Theatre ahead, in Townend Bank, 1925.

Her Majesty's Theatre,
Proprietors—THE WALSALL THEATRES Co., Ltd.

ONCE NIGHTLY SEASON.
Prices of Admission :
Reserved Seats (Tax included) :
PRIVATE BOXES 21/- (to hold 4 persons).
STALLS 3/6 and 2/4.
CIRCLE 3/6 and 3/-.
Unreserved (Tax included) :
PIT 1/3, Early Door 1/6.
GALLERY 8d., Early Door 11d.
Children's Prices :
Full Price at Evening Performances.
Special Matinee Prices, as follow
DRESS CIRCLE 1/10 and 1/6.
ORCHESTRA STALLS 1/10 and 1/3.
PIT 8d., Early Door 9d.
All Tax included.
Private Boxes, also all Circle and Stalls Seats Booked in Advance.
Box Office open Daily from 10 a.m. to 1 p.m. 6 p.m. to 7 p.m
and from 8 p.m. to 9 p.m
Seats Booked by Telephone are liable to be sold if not paid for half-an-hour before performance commences.
Seats not guaranteed unless Booked.
Telephone 245.

The Management reserve the right to refuse admission. Tradesmen are requested not to supply goods to theatre without printed order signed by the Manager.

General Manager .. Mr. William Joseph Andrews
Acting Manager .. . Mr. William Tennant
Musical Director .. Mr. G. Blakemore

THEATRE DIARY.

November 1st—LILAC TIME.
No. 1 Company with Courtice Pounds.

November 8—THE FARMER'S WIFE.
Delightful Comedy.

November 15—THE RIGHT AGE TO MARRY. Lancashire Play.

November 22 THE STREET SINGER.
Musical Play.

November 29—YVONNE.
Daly's Theatre Musical Play.

December 6—THE GIRL IN THE TAXI.

Special Note.
Monday and Tuesday, December 20 and 21. at 7-30 p.m. Mr. Cartwright and friends present "FRENCH LEAVE," in aid of Victoria Nursing Institute.
11.10.26

Wednesbury Hippodrome, 2nd March 1950.

The Empire Theatre, Freer Street, 1959.

The Dale Cinema, New Road/Walsall Street, Willenhall, 1933.

The Gaumont Cinema, Lower Bridge Street, 1948.

Savoy Cinema, Townend, 1949.

The Palace Cinema, The Old Square, 27th September 1949.

Magician Mike Gancia, a great favourite with Walsall club audiences.

Walsall Observer, Friday, October 9, 1970.

Contralto Margaret Lowe, "A Voice of Rare Quality".

13.5.44

WEEK-END RADIO

TONIGHT

HOME SERVICE

6—News. 6.30. The World Goes By. 7, Light Orchestra : Iris Loveridge, piano. 7.45. The Week in Westminster : Beverley Baxter, M.P. 8, Vaudeville of 1944; £100 Red Cross Contest. 9. News. 9.20. Alastair Sim in The Anatomist. by James Bridie. 10.35. Prayers. 10.50. Dance Music. 12-12.20. News.

GENERAL FORCES

6—Shipmates Ashore. 6.30. Atlantic Spotlight. 7. News. 7.10. News from Canada. 7.15. Gramo : Forces Favourites. 7.45. Band. 8.15. Football Results. 8.30. B.B.C. Symphony Orchestra. 9. News. 9.5. Replies to Letters. 9.15. Association Football. 9.30. Programme for British Forces in West Africa. 10. Johnny Canuck's Revue. 10.30. Melville Christie's Dance Orchestra. 10.59-11, News Headlines.

TOMORROW

HOME SERVICE

7—News. 7.15. Gramo : Orchestra. 7.45. Band. 8.15. Gramo : Concerto's Progress. 9. News. 9.30. Service. 10.15. G. D. Cunningham, organ. 10.30. Orchestra. 11. Music Lover's Calendar. 11.20. Gramo : Bizet. 12. Light Orchestra. 12.50. Films : Dilys Powell. 1. News. 1.15. Russian Commentary : Alexander Werth. 1.30. Gramo : Elgar. 1.45. Radio Allotment. 2. Orchestra. 2.30. Louis Kentner, piano. 3. Band. 3.30. London Symphony Orchestra: Nicholas Medtner, piano. 4.30. The Anvil. 5. News (Welsh). 5.5. Programme in Welsh. 5.20. Children. 6. News. 6.30. Transatlantic Call : People to People. 7. The Shipowner : Talk by J. A. Billmer. 7.15. Grand Hotel. 8. Service. 8.40. Appeal on behalf of the Lebanon Hospital for Mental Diseases, by Sir Ronald Storrs. 8.45. Home Guard Sunday. 9. News; Postcript. 9.30. Adventures of Don Quixote. 10.5. Homage to Johann Strauss. 11.5. Hirsch String Quartet. 11.30. Gramo : Bach. Stokowski. 12-12.20. News.

GENERAL FORCES

6.30—News. 6.42. Gramo. 7. News Headlines : Gramo. 8. News. 8.15. Gramo. 9. News. 9.15. Messages from Overseas. 10.15. Service. 10.30. Sunday Serenade. 11.10. Greetings from East Africa. 11.30. Calling Canadians. 12. News Headlines : Newsletter. 12.15. Felix Mendelssohn's Hawaiian Serenaders. 12.30. Service. 1. News. 1.15. Kay Cavendish. 1.30. Brains Trust. 2. News Headlines : Orchestral and Choral Music. 2.30. The Speaking Clock, by John Dickson Carr. 3. News. 3.10. Gramo : Forces Favourites. 3.30. Newsreel. 3.45. Football Results. 3.59. News Headlines. 4. Palestine Half-Hour. 4.30. I.T.M.A. 5. News. 5.15. John Brophy on Books. 8.30. Fred Hartley. 6. Variety Band-Box. 7. News. 7.10. News from Canada. 7.15. Gramo : Forces Favourites. 8. Calling Malta. 8.30. Palace of Varieties. 9. News : Parliamentary Summary. 9.15. Community Hymn-Singing. 9.45. Chappell's Queen's Hall Light Orchestra. 10.25. Epilogue. 10.30. Sextet. 10.59-11, News Headlines.

The Garnett Orton Concert Party, c. 1942.

Carl Wynne and his Band, Town Hall, 1944.

Guests at Walsall Harmonic Society's Ladies' Evening, the Kenmare Restaurant, Bridge Street, March 1973.

The AFS (Auxiliary Fire Service) Dance Band, Town Hall, 1941.

LOCAL CHARACTERS

Film and TV character actor Richard Wattis, born in Hollies Drive, Wednesbury, went on to star in such films as "Hobson Choice" and "Simon and Laura" and was a regular in the television series "Sykes" through the sixties.

...rome K Jerome, author of "Three Men in a Boat", ...ecame an Honorary Freeman of the Borough on 17th ...ebruary 1927.

...ctor Frank Windsor, educated at Queen Mary's ...rammar School, star of TV's "Z-Cars", "Flying Lady", ...c.

Wednesbury-born Janice Nicholls, who came to fame in the television series "Thank Your Lucky Stars", along with her husband Brian Meacham, meets the Beatles, 8th April 1965. She is best remembered for her catchphrase "Oi'll Give It Foive!."

THE CATCHPHRASE "Not Now, Arthur," has been reverberating around millions of homes during the latest series of BBC's Morecambe and Wise Show, and the man who has never yet been able to play a complete tune on his harmonica is Arthur Tolcher. of Bloxwich, who this year will be appearing in his 18th Derek Salberg pantomime at the Alexandra Theatre in Birmingham

Will he be playing the harmonica during the pantomime? Arthur won't say, but he will be displaying his amazing versatility by portraying two characters in the pantomime, King Richard and Friar Tuck.

Without doubt this has been Arthur's most successful year. To appear in a series of six shows with Britain's most famous comedy duo is quite a coup, but how did he manage to get such a prestigious booking?

Bachelor Arthur, who lives with his 83-year-old mother in Tolcher Towers — a council house in Bloxwich — talked to me about his early connections with Eric and Ernie.

"I first met Ernie Wise in 1939," he said. "We were both in the show Bandwagon at the London Palladium.   9.12.74

Arthur Tolcher

Ken Rattenbury, jazz trumpeter.

TV Presenter, Bob Warman, launches a video production contest with the help of Walsall school children, Mark and Stella Taylor, 30th October 1986.

Actress Sue Nicholls (on right), who plays the character Audrey Roberts in "Coronation Street". With her is Mavis, played by Thelma Barlow, May 1987

THE TOWN CENTRE

Perhaps the logical place to begin our introduction to the items in this chapter is at The Bridge. Why is it called The Bridge, anyway? No river or stream can be seen today but a brook, a principal tributary of the River Tame, ran through this area and was referred to as "Walsall Water". It was entirely open, wide, shallow and liable to sudden flooding. It divided Digbeth from Park Street and was crossed only by a foot-bridge but, when flooding occurred, ladies (for a fare of one penny) were carried across on ponies which were stabled at the nearby New Inn. The brook was culverted over in 1813. Maybe there is some connection here with adjoining Digbeth, a name probably derived from the Anglo-Saxon "dic" (a dyke) and "paeth" (a path).

Rushall Street, once a main street, had large residential houses, the ancestral homes of many old Walsall families. William Siddons, who became the husband of the famous actress, Sarah, was born at a small inn there. Halfway along the street stood the Ware well, perpetuated by the name of a nearby street.

From its prominence and make-up, Church Hill, a mass of limestone, could easily have been a fortified post in early times and Ablewell (Avalwall) and the Ditch (Dyche) suggest that this area might once have been surrounded by a fosse or moat.

The locality of Fieldgate, between New Street and Bath Street, once formed the southern limit of the town and gives some idea of the small size of old Walsall. Bath Street itself was aptly named: baths were formerly situated close by.

The Bridge, 1924.

Lower Bridge Street, 1926.

The George Hotel, The Bridge, with Digbeth on the right, 21st June 1935.

Wisemore/Stafford Street, 1936.

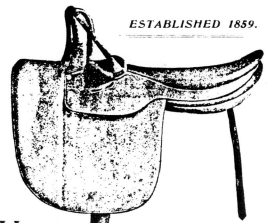

The Market, 1951.

The Bridge, Digbeth/Bradford Street, June 1953.

The Bridge, 25th March 1954.

A tanker waits to turn right into Park Street from The Bridge, 23rd October 1967.

A spectacular birds-eye view, with Digbeth in the foreground, 1955.

Park Street, in the days when pedestrianisation was just an idea, 4th July 1972.

OUT AND ABOUT

Walsall is surrounded on its southern and western borders by a network of manufacturing towns and districts of which Elihu Burritt, an American Consul, said in the late 19th century, "they form a green velvet binding". According to Burritt again, to the east and north there are "fine stretches of open and elevated country, almost unequalled in England". It is still possible to share his views today. There are woods, lakes and commons stretching for miles, with Barr Beacon, a fine public open space, easily accessible from the centre of Walsall. Great Barr Hall was once the seat of Lady Bateman and Scott. Do we see a connection here with the public-house and district known to many as "The Scott Arms", at the nearby junction of Newton Road, Birmingham Road, Queslett Road and Walsall Road? Further north are the pleasant areas of Aldridge, Stonnall, Shenstone and others, eventually leading to Brownhills, Chasewater and that vast region of natural beauty, Cannock Chase.

The Queen visits the Crabtree works, 24th May 1962.

3.10.70

One-man buses for Walsall

One-man bus services are to be launched in Walsall next week on certain routes.

They start on Sunday on service numbers 35 and 49—covering Pleck, Inner Circle, Goscote, Blakenall and Bloxwich districts.

This will be followed up the following Saturday on service number 9, the Walsall Wood — Shenstone route.

Fares have been revised to make for easier handling and passengers are to be introduced to a new self-service system.

The Walsall Observer

AND
SOUTH STAFFORDSHIRE CHRONICLE.

LARGEST CERTIFIED NET SALE
OF ALL
STAFFORDSHIRE WEEKLIES.

AD OFFICE.—"Observer" Buildings, Bridge Street. Walsall.
Telephone : Walsall 2137, 2138, 2139.

Leamore Methodist Youth Club, August 1944.

Alfred Street, Bloxwich, 9th September 1952.

Bloxwich Civic Sunday, 7th June 1964.

High Street, Aldridge, 25th August 1956.

89

The Queen leaves Sutton Park after the Scout's Jamboree, 3rd August 1957.

A pre-fabricated footbridge in the course of erection, High Street, Walsall Wood, 10th April 1951.

THE LETTERS OF ANUK

15/2/52

By

TOM H. TOWNSON.

Birthdays

DEAR Ali,
As it ever occaerred to yer thot if yo'd never 'ad no baerthday you udn't be 'ere? Well, it's right. Ar, you con tek it from me thot baerthdays am very importont things.

Unless yo've got a baerthday yo cor get yer life insured cos they always wanten to know when yo was born. Ar, an' in yower case they'd also probobly wanten to know why yo was born.

Yo've 'aeard o' Mrs. Crumble as lives nayer we? Well, it was 'er baerthday yesterday. Although 'er never smokes, 'er's very fond o' the smell o' bacca. In the caercumstonces thot Scotch bloke as lodges wie 'er bought 'er a pipe for a baerthday present. 'E tode 'er thot if 'er ud paerchase some bacca an' find some motches 'e'd smoke it for 'er while 'er sat an' sniffed.

Don't mention this to our Baertha in case it puts ideas into 'er yed. Ar, I con see 'er buyin' me a pair o' them nylons an' then offerin' to wear 'em for me.

High Street, Walsall Wood, 1928.

High Street, Brownhills, c. 1905.

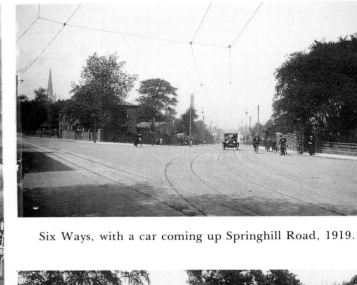

Six Ways, with a car coming up Springhill Road, 1919.

Cannock Road, running through the centre of Brownhills, 6th May 1965.

Park Hall Estate, 28th July 1976.

King Street, from Bull Stake, Darlaston, 11th March 1953.

93

Darlaston, with the Parish Church of St Lawrence just left of centre, 11th October 1963.

The Duke and Duchess of Gloucester visit the Rubery Owen Day Nursery, Darlaston, 1943. The Duke is in military uniform and the Duchess has just been presented with a bouquet.

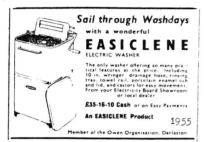

Wednesbury Market Place, 1930.

Walsall Street, looking towards Willenhall Market Place, March 1925.

Willenhall Memorial Park, 31st January 1956.

Willenhall Carnival, 29th May 1965.

25th April 1950.

THE
ARBORETUM

Visitors admire the new Cupid Fountain, 10th July 1951.

The Illuminations, described by the Mayor, Alderman Thompson as "the best free show in the Midlands", 5th September 1967. The cost — £10,000, almost all of it provided by donations.

3rd September 1973.

ACKNOWLEDGEMENTS

(for providing photographs, for encouragement and numerous other favours)

Neil Allen; Birmingham Post and Mail Ltd; Birmingham Reference Library, Local Studies; Bloxwich Golf Club; Val Bradley; British Red Cross (Walsall); Anne Burton; Arthur Camwell; Dave Carpenter; Jackie Cash; Margery Chell; Jabez Cliff & Co.; Crabtree Electrical Industries Ltd.; Janet Dance; George Dennis; Harry Granger; Jack Haddock; Clive Hardy; Geoff Hawkins; John Haycock; Betty Hodson; Robert Holmes; George Hughes; Anne Jennings; Daisy Jowett; Cyril Keay; Norman Kenyon; Sid Lloyd; John Lote; Tom Luck; McKechnie Extruded Products; Philip Murphy; Terry Owles; Mary Pearson; Debbie Perry; Victor Price; Joan Rathbone; Ken Rattenbury; Liz Rees; Salvation Army Members (Walsall); Reg Sanders; Freda Shaw; Ralph Smith; Tan and Edgar Smith; Captain Nigel Tansley; Janet and Brian Thompson; Albert and Doris Tinkler; Walsall Central Library, Information Services Dept.; Walsall Leather Centre Museum; Walsall Observer; Stanley Webb; Wednesbury Library; Ed Wilkes; Sam Williams; Ray Wilson; Wolverhampton Library; Beryl Wright; Carl Wynne.

Please forgive any possible omissions. Every effort has been made to include all organisations and individuals involved in the book.